American
AIR FORCES
in the Vietnam War

HUNTER KEETER

WORLD ALMANAC® LIBRARY

Please visit our web site at: www.worldalmanaclibrary.com
For a free color catalog describing World Almanac® Library's list of high-quality books and multimedia programs, call 1-800-848-2928 (USA) or 1-800-387-3178 (Canada). World Almanac® Library's fax: (414) 332-3567.

Library of Congress Cataloging-in-Publication Data

Keeter, Hunter.
 American air forces in the Vietnam War / by Hunter Keeter.
    p. cm. — (The American experience in Vietnam)
 Includes bibliographical references and index.
 ISBN 0-8368-5773-9 (lib. bdg.)
 ISBN 0-8368-5780-1 (softcover)
 1. Vietnamese Conflict, 1961-1975—Aerial operations, American—Juvenile literature.
 2. United States—Air Force—History—Vietnamese Conflict, 1961-1975—Juvenile literature.
 I. Title. II. Series.
 DS558.8.K44   2005
 959.704'348—dc22   2004058091

First published in 2005 by
World Almanac® Library
330 West Olive Street, Suite 100
Milwaukee, WI 53212 USA

Copyright © 2005 by World Almanac® Library.

Developed by Amber Books Ltd.
Editor: James Bennett
Designer: Colin Hawes
Photo research: Natasha Jones
World Almanac® Library editors: Mark Sachner and Alan Wachtel
World Almanac® Library art direction: Tammy West
World Almanac® Library production: Jessica Morris

Picture Acknowledgements
Aerospace Publishing: 12, 14, 20, 22, 23, 28, 34; Camera Press: 37; Cody Images (www.codyimages.com): cover (top left), 9, 15, 27, 32, 38, 40; Corbis: cover (main), 1, 4 (top left), 6, 8, 11, 16, 17, 19, 24, 26, 30, 31, 36, 39, 43; U.S. National Archives: 13.

Printed in Canada

1 2 3 4 5 6 7 8 9 09 08 07 06 05

About the Author

HUNTER KEETER is a journalist with *Defense Daily*, a leading defense business publication. He is the author of the *Homeland Security* and *U.S. Marines* volumes in the *America's Armed Forces* series from World Almanac® Library. Before becoming a writer, he earned an MA in Literature and Education and worked as a schoolteacher. He lives in Arlington, Virginia.

Table of Contents

Words that appear in the glossary are printed in **boldface** type the first time they occur in the text

Introduction

The Vietnam War (1954–1975) was part of a larger conflict known as the Second Indochina War, which raged in Southeast Asia and involved the nations of Cambodia, Laos, and Vietnam. From 1946 until 1954, the Vietnamese had fought for independence from France during the First Indochina War. When the French were defeated, the country was divided into North and South Vietnam. Vietnamese communists controlled North Vietnam and wanted to unify Vietnam under communist rule. Non-communist Vietnamese controlled the South. In the 1950s, the United States and the Soviet Union were in the early years of their struggle over political, economic, and military influence in various parts of the world. Known as the Cold War, this struggle did not pit each nation against the other directly. Rather, each supported other countries that were squared off against one another. In the mid-1950s, the U.S. began training South Vietnam's army, while the Soviet Union and China backed communist North Vietnam. By the mid-1960s, U.S. forces fought alongside the Army of the Republic of Vietnam (ARVN) against the North Vietnamese Army (NVA) and the National Front for the Liberation of Vietnam (NLF).

Airpower was the defining feature of the Vietnam War, with Air Force, Navy, Marine Corps, and Army forces contributing pilots and aircraft. The experiences of U.S. pilots in Vietnam varied. Some Air Force and Navy aviators flew supersonic jet fighters, battling North Vietnamese pilots in ferocious dogfights. Other pilots flew slower, propeller-driven planes, braving danger on low-altitude observation, attack, rescue, and resupply missions.

One of the most successful U.S. fighter jets flown during the Vietnam War was the F-4 Phantom II, which could fly at more than twice the speed of sound. Vietnam also was known as the "helicopter war" because hundreds of Army and Marine Corps utility and attack "choppers" were involved in the fighting. Helicopters added a vertical dimension to **infantry** fighting tactics whereby infantry could be landed behind and around an enemy to attack from all sides.

The mightiest airborne firepower came from Air Force bomber planes: the Air Force's B-52 Stratofortress and F-105 Thunderchief bombers. Bomber crewmen were in constant danger from surface-to-air missiles and antiaircraft **artillery** shells that could tear their planes apart. Additionally, bomber crewmen had to be on guard against North Vietnamese MiG interceptor aircraft.

When a U.S. aircraft came under attack and was hit, the pilot had just seconds to react. Sometimes, the pilot had no choice but to eject and parachute away from his plane before it crashed. When this happened, the pilot's prospects were grim. If he managed to parachute safely to the ground, the pilot then had to face the danger of being killed or captured by enemy forces. If he failed to escape and evade capture, the pilot could expect a long confinement at a military prison, such as the infamous "Hanoi Hilton." A large number of U.S. aviators were held captive in North Vietnam, some for several years.

Below: This map shows North and South Vietnam and the surrounding area. Key regions, cities, and military bases are indicated.

5

CHAPTER 1: Jet Fighter Pilots

Fast Movers

Right: U.S. Navy A-4 Skyhawk pilots walk back to squadron HQ aboard their aircraft carrier. After missions, aircrew often met with intelligence officers, who debriefed them about their missions, learning information crucial to the planning of future operations.

From bases in South Vietnam and Thailand, and aboard aircraft carriers at sea, U.S. Navy and Air Force pilots flew state-of-the-art fighter jets—planes such as the F-4 Phantom II, the F-8 Crusader, and the F-5 Freedom Fighter. The pilots who flew combat air patrol missions dueled with North Vietnamese air force pilots, who flew Chinese- and Soviet-built planes, such as the MiG-21.

Of all the U.S. fighter jets flown during the Vietnam War, perhaps the best known and most successful was the F-4 Phantom II. The F-4 was a powerful fighter that could fly at more than twice the speed of sound. The speed of sound at sea level is about 750 miles (1,200 kilometers) per hour. The Phantom II carried AIM-7 radar-guided missiles and AIM-9 heat-seeking missiles.

High above Vietnam, jets screamed through the air at more than 600 miles (966 km) per hour during dogfights. A dogfight is a fight between two or more fighter planes, usually at close range. Such contests were great tests of skill, with the pilots turning and accelerating, trying to catch each other off guard. Sometimes, opposing planes in a dogfight passed so closely that their pilots reported seeing one another's faces through their Plexiglas canopies. Such high-speed maneuvers during aerial combat put tremendous strain on a pilot's body. This strain—not unlike the sensation one feels when turning sharply on a roller coaster

ACES OF THE VIETNAM WAR

Between 1965 and 1973, five F-4 Phantom II aviators achieved "Ace" status for shooting down five or more enemy planes in aerial combat. The U.S aces of the Vietnam War were Air Force Captain Charles E. DeBellevue, with six "kills" as a weapon systems operator; Air Force Captain Richard S. Ritchie, with five kills as a pilot; Air Force Captain Jeffery S. Feinstein, with five kills as a weapon systems operator; Navy Lieutenant Randall "Duke" Cunningham, with five kills as a pilot; and Navy Lieutenant (Junior Grade) William "Irish" Driscoll, with five kills as a radar intercept officer.

ride—is measured in "gravities," or "g." One g is equal to the normal force of Earth's gravity, and two gs is equal to twice the force of Earth's gravity.

HIGH-SPEED COMBAT

Flying patrols in the two-seat F-4 against MiGs was physically and mentally demanding. An F-4 fighter pilot had to be alert and awake every second during a dogfight. A lapse of attention, even for a second, could mean destruction for the F-4 and death or capture for its crew. A physically fit pilot's body can tolerate about nine g for short periods of time. The danger in combat from excessive g-force, or even negative g-force—experienced when falling downhill on a roller coaster ride—is that it draws blood from the brain, which can cause unconsciousness. A g-force-induced blackout could cause the pilot to lose control of the plane. To prevent blackouts, pilots wore one-piece g-suits that laced close to their bodies. The g-suit would be automatically filled with compressed air during high-speed maneuvers,

Below: U.S. pilots flew multirole planes—such as this Navy F-4B Phantom II of Fighter Squadron VF-96 from the USS *Enterprise*—that were equally capable of air-to-air combat and ground attack.

A NAVAL AVIATOR EARNS HIS ACE

On May 10, 1972, U.S. Representative Randall Cunningham was a naval aviator on his three hundredth mission over Vietnam.

"I downed three North Vietnamese MiGs that day; together with the two I had previously shot down, I had just become the first U.S. Navy ace of the Vietnam War," Cunningham said on October 26, 1999, at a ceremony on Capitol Hill marking the 50th anniversary of the Geneva Conventions.

"I was making the turn back home when, forty miles inland, my F-4 was severely damaged by an enemy surface-to-air missile. I barrel-rolled that airplane until we reached the mouth of the Red River. My radar intercept officer, Willie Driscoll, and I ejected just as the Phantom II exploded."

Left: Some aircraft, such as this F-4 flown by Navy aces Cunningham and Driscoll, demanded the attention of two men. The pilot sat in the front seat and concentrated on flying, pursuing targets, and evading danger. The radar intercept officer in the rear seat managed the F-4's complex weapon system.

squeezing the pilot's legs and abdomen, so blood could not rush from his head.

F-4 crews often had to perform high-speed maneuvers as they faced enemy pilots flying powerful jets such as the MiG-21. The silver MiGs were heavily armed for close air-to-air combat with 1.18-inch (30-mm) cannon and "Atoll" heat-seeking missiles. Until later models were modified to carry cannon pods, the F-4 was armed solely with missiles, a fact that some pilots said put the Phantom II at a disadvantage in a dogfight with MiGs.

While high-performance fighters like the F-4 and F-8 were designed for combat air patrol, these and other fast movers often flew close air support missions, using bombs, rockets, and guns to defend friendly troops on the ground. For example, on strike missions, the F-4 carried twice the normal bomb load of a World War II-era B-17 Flying Fortress bomber.

CARRIER BASES

Naval aviators launched and landed their planes aboard aircraft carriers at Yankee Station, a location in the Gulf of Tonkin off the coast of North Vietnam, or at Dixie Station, off South Vietnam. They got into the air by taking a "cat shot," a catapult launch from an aircraft carrier. During a launch, a steam-powered piston attached to the jet's nosewheel shot down a track under the carrier's flight deck. The piston slung the plane off the ship's bow (the front of the ship) and into the air. To land his jet aboard the carrier, the naval aviator lined up on the ship's stern (the rear of the ship) and lowered his arrestor hook (a steel hook hinged to the jet's tail). Looking through his cockpit at a lighted display on the carrier's stern, called the Fresnel Lens Landing System, the naval aviator centered the light on his airplane's nose. This alignment was referred to as "calling the ball." As a circular icon in the pilot's **head-up display** came to rest on the flight deck, the naval aviator radioed the carrier and announced his readiness to land.

The aircraft carrier had heavy-gauge braided steel cables stretched across the stern end of its flight deck. A naval aviator brought his plane down hard, slamming onto the deck and catching one of the cables with his jet's arrestor hook. In this maneuver, called a "trap," the fighter's landing speed changed from more than 150 miles (241 km) per hour to zero miles per hour in a 1.2-second, heart-pounding lunge.

F-5 FREEDOM FIGHTER

Some U.S. and South Vietnamese air force pilots flew the F-5 Freedom Fighter, which was a good aircraft for close-air support

Below: Flight operations were a grueling, round-the-clock effort. These Navy aviation **ordnance** men are wheeling 500-pound (227-kilogram) bombs to a waiting line of A-4 Skyhawk fighter-bombers.

Right: Because calls for action could mean a rapid "scramble" for pilots to get airborne, attack planes like this F-5 Freedom Fighter were kept fueled, armed, and ready.

missions. The twin-engine F-5 was a slender plane armed with two 0.79-inch (20-mm) cannon and carried rockets, bombs, or air-to-air missiles. F-5 pilots often carried napalm canisters during close-air support missions. Napalm is a sticky, **incendiary** mixture of jellied fuel that sticks to its target and can ignite huge fires to destroy or drive away enemy ground troops.

Flying close air support attack runs in low-level formations required F-5 pilots to have a good grasp of geometry. During a napalm strike, a flight of four F-5s lined up an attack run along the best approach to an enemy unit. The planes flew in at low altitude, skimming the treetops. When an imaginary line between the jets and the targets on the ground was at the correct angle, the pilots released their bombs and pulled away. Through the rearview mirrors inside their canopies, the F-5 pilots watched their napalm canisters tumble to the ground behind their planes and erupt in sheets of flame.

"BLACK MAN AND ROBIN"

General Daniel "Chappie" James, Jr., (1920–1978) was an F-4 Phantom II pilot during the Vietnam War and the first African American four-star general. James was vice-commander under Colonel Robin Olds of the Eighth Tactical Fighter Wing at Ubon Royal Thai Air Force Base, Thailand. James described his partnership with Olds as "Black Man and Robin," referring to popular 1960s television and comic book superheroes Batman and Robin. James, who also flew during World War II (1939–1945) and the Korean War (1950–1953), had a black panther painted on his flight helmet. On January 2, 1967, Black Man and Robin led their wing in Operation Bolo, battling North Vietnamese MiGs. During Operation Bolo, F-4s shot down seven MiG-21s, the largest tally of any single mission during the Vietnam War.

Left: After the Vietnam War, "Chappie" James became the first African American four-star general in the U.S. Air Force.

CHAPTER 2: Propeller Aircraft Pilots

Low and Slow

Right: Forward air controllers, such as this OV-10 pilot, were vital to deep strike and close air support missions. Not only did the controllers help target enemy forces and direct attacks, these pilots also assessed damage and provided valuable intelligence data.

The landscape of Southeast Asia was mountainous and thickly forested. The climate was warm and humid for most of the year, with heavy rainfall between May and October. Much of the landscape was a patchwork of farming villages and paddies—flooded rice fields separated by raised dikes.

The pilots who had the best vantage point to see what was happening on the ground were forward air controllers. These pilots flew "low and slow" propeller-driven planes, such as the Cessna O-2 Skymaster. Their missions were to scout an enemy force and coordinate air attacks upon it. An O-2 pilot flew into North Vietnamese-controlled territory and looked for targets. When he sighted an enemy troop column, vehicle convoy, or encampment, the O-2 pilot (forward air controller) radioed ground-based Sky Spot radar stations to arrange a bombing mission. The Sky Spot tracked bombers, which were flying high over the clouds. When the O-2, which was beneath the clouds, radioed in a target's map coordinates, the radar crew told the bombers exactly when to release their weapons. The bomber crews might not have even seen their targets, but the forward air controller directed

OPERATION RANCH HAND

Between 1962 and 1971, Air Force pilots flew twin-engine C-123 cargo planes in Operation Ranch Hand, a plan to air-drop chemicals to clear roads of jungle undergrowth and destroy farm crops that were believed to be used by enemy troops. During Ranch Hand, the C-123 pilots sprayed about 19 million gallons (72 million liters) of herbicide. According to U.S. Air Force reports, about 11 million gallons (42 million liters) of the chemicals used during Ranch Hand included "Agent Orange," which contained poisonous compounds called dioxins. In 2000, an Air Force study reported that there was a link between exposure to Agent Orange and serious human health problems, such as diabetes.

the attack with such pinpoint accuracy that the bomber crews didn't need to see them.

An O-2 flying low and slow was well within range of North Vietnamese Army (NVA) rifles, machine guns, and antiaircraft artillery fire. Of the twelve Congressional Medals of Honor awarded to airmen during the Vietnam War, forward air controller pilots earned three.

CARGO CARRIERS

Slow movers fulfilled other important roles during the Vietnam War. Air Force, Marine Corps, and Coast Guard pilots flew unarmed cargo planes, such as the rugged C-130 Hercules, carrying supplies and fuel and transporting troops into combat zones. Pilots who flew supply missions often had to land on short, rough runways at remote bases.

In 1965, Air Force C-130s moved from bases in Japan to Tan Son Nhut Airport, near Saigon. The C-130 crews supported the buildup of Marines at Da Nang and Army cavalry troopers

Below: Transport planes like this C-130 Hercules were never more vulnerable than while sitting on the ground unloading their cargo. The crews of these planes often kept their engines running, allowing a fast takeoff if they were threatened by enemy artillery.

elsewhere in South Vietnam during 1965. In 1968, Air Force and
Marine Corps C–130 pilots brought fuel, ammunition, food, and
medical supplies to the isolated Marine Combat Base Khe Sanh.
The NVA laid siege to the base, cutting off about six thousand
Marines and pounding the troops with heavy artillery fire.
Transport pilots landed on the dirt strip at Khe Sanh, often taking
hits from the mortar bombs and shells the NVA threw into the
camp as they flew in and out. Eventually, a force of Marines and
other troops reached Khe Sanh and lifted the siege after seventy-
seven days.

ATTACK MISSIONS

Not every propeller aircraft pilot flew unarmed into danger. Some U.S. and South Vietnamese pilots flew heavily armed A-1 Skyraiders, planes that could give back the punishment they took. A-1 pilots flew attack and rescue missions across Southeast Asia. The Air Force pilots who flew Skyraiders were fond of its armament, which included four 0.79-inch (20-mm) cannon and many bombs and rockets. Despite being almost twenty years old when the Vietnam War began, the Skyraider was essential to U.S. operations in Southeast Asia. No other plane carried such a variety of weapons, or endured such long flights at low altitude, or was subjected to as much enemy fire, as the reliable old A-1.

On attack missions, A-1 pilots often struck the NVA and NLF along the Ho Chi Minh Trail. The trail was a 12,000-mile (19,312-km) path snaking along the mountainous border shared by Cambodia, Laos, and Vietnam. The trail was a key target because it was important to the success of North Vietnam's war effort. The NVA and NLF used the Ho Chi Minh Trail to transport troops and more than 1.3 million tons (1.2 million metric tons) of supplies between 1962 and 1975.

SEARCH AND RESCUE

The A-1 Skyraider was also used for search-and-rescue missions, which sometimes reached far behind enemy lines into North Vietnam. In hostile territory, surrounded by NVA or NLF forces, the heavily armed A-1 pilots escorted HH-3 helicopters to retrieve downed airmen. One famous rescue occurred in June 1972, when A-1s and helicopters brought Air Force Captain Roger C. Locher of Sabetha, Kansas, back from North Vietnam.

Locher was a weapon systems operator in the back seat of an F-4 piloted by Major Robert A. Lodge. Their plane was the lead jet of four in a flight code-named "Oyster." On May 10, 1972,

Oyster Flight flew into North Vietnam looking for possible targets. Thirty miles (48 km) west of Hanoi, the F-4s came across a flight of North Vietnamese MiG-21s setting up an ambush for U.S. bombers heading north during Operation Linebacker, a U.S. bombing campaign that attacked targets in the north, such as airfields, power plants, and radio stations, thereby disrupting the flow of supplies and reinforcements to North Vietnamese units fighting in the South.

Within moments of the F-4 pilots engaging the MiG-21s, three of the enemy aircraft took missile hits and fell from the sky. Oyster One, Locher and Lodge's plane, maneuvered onto the tail of the fourth MiG-21. Intent on catching the MiG, Locher and Lodge did not see a second group of North Vietnamese jets

Below: A Navy AD-4 Skyraider waits its turn on the steam-powered launch catapult aboard the aircraft carrier USS *Coral Sea.*

Above: Air Force special operations planes, such as this A-1H/J Skyraider, patrolled the skies over Vietnam to aid in the rescue of downed aviators and embattled infantry units.

coming up behind them. In moments, the tables were turned. A Chinese-built Shenyang J-6 fighter fired two bursts from its three 1.18-inch (30-mm) cannon. The explosive shells blasted through the Phantom II's **fuselage** and starboard (right) wing, smashing an engine and blowing out the jet's hydraulic system. Oyster One lost control and plummeted to the ground from a height of 7,000 feet (2,134 meters). No one saw Locher fire his ejection seat and rocket away from the F-4 before impact. Lodge probably died in the crash.

By June 1, 1972, everyone assumed Locher also had died. That was the day he radioed for help from deep in the forest. Locher was hiding 5 miles (8 km) from Yen Bai Airfield, North Vietnam. He had evaded capture for twenty-two days, fewer than 100 miles (160 km) north of Hanoi. Yen Bai Airfield was located in a heavily defended area. The U.S. pilots who heard Locher's radio call knew that a rescue mission would be risky.

A-1 Skyraider pilots from the First Special Operations Squadron based at Nakhon Phanom Royal Thai Air Base, Thailand, planned the mission. A flight of Skyraiders, waiting on the airfield, roared into life and took off, leading HH-53 helicopters (known as "Jolly Green Giants" after a cartoon character made popular during the 1960s) into North Vietnam. Rescue missions in enemy territory required courage and teamwork. Each member of the four-man rescue team had a call sign to identify himself on the radio. A-1 pilots had the call sign "Sandy" due to their sand-colored camouflage. Ahead of the helicopters, two of the A-1s flew low to the ground, so their pilots could watch for trouble. The other two A-1s stayed a few miles away from the rescue site, flying in a protective circle around two Jolly Green Giants.

Air Force Captain Ron Smith led the Sandy pilots who flew into North Vietnam after Locher on June 1, 1972. The Sandys tried to locate Locher's exact position using an electronic automatic direction-finding device, which homed in on a signal from a downed aviator's radio. The rescuers met tough resistance, however, before they found Locher's hiding place among the bamboo thickets and underbrush. Traveling through the valleys and over the ridges near Hanoi, the A-1s were hit by NVA infantry rifle and machine gun fire and 0.9-inch (23-mm) antiaircraft artillery.

LOW, SLOW, AND DANGEROUS

Flying tactical aircraft close to the ground was dangerous work, according to Air Force A-1 Skyraider pilot Captain Byron E. Hukee.

During a mission, Hukee dropped his bombs and pulled his plane away, heading for a mountain ridge. He looked back to see his bombs explode. Suddenly, he found himself flying into thick fog. Hukee could no longer see how far away he was from the mountainside and was concerned he might crash into it.

"I climbed as high as possible," Hukee wrote. "I had the sick feeling that the elevation gain was not enough, but I was committed. After what seemed like an eternity, I broke out above the clouds."

AIR FORCE GUNSHIPS

Between 1964 and 1969, Air Force pilots flew AC-47 "Spooky" gunships. The C-47 had been designed for cargo and paratroop transport during World War II. During the Vietnam War, however, the Air Force created the AC-47 by adding three 0.3-inch (7.62-mm) General Electric SUU-11A miniguns. Each minigun could shoot six thousand bullets per minute. Other gunships were developed using C-130s, which carried a 4.1-inch (105-mm) howitzer for tank-busting missions. To U.S and allied ground troops, the gunships were guardian angels. To the enemy, however, a gunship prowling the night sky was called a "thug."

Above: A heavily armed AC-47 "Spooky" gunship.

The Skyraiders could withstand the fire, but the Jolly Greens were vulnerable. Suddenly, a MiG-21 roared past the rescue helicopters. There was too much danger to bring Locher home. Smith ordered his fellow Sandy pilots and the Jolly Greens to regroup and head back to Thailand. A second rescue mission was planned for the next day. On June 2, 1972, a new mission rounded up 119 aircraft, including A-1s, HH-53 choppers, a C-130 equipped to refuel the helicopters, and F-4s to defend against MiGs and to attack ground targets.

The race was on to reach Locher before he was captured. The F-4s and other attack jets struck Yen Bai Airfield and the nearby antiaircraft artillery sites in an attempt to divert the North Vietnamese away from the mission. The A-1s came in next, dropping bombs and **strafing** the NVA soldiers closing in on Locher. As the F-4s arrived to suppress the NVA troops, the HH-53 Jolly Green crews flew in to make the rescue. Inside the HH-53s were Air Force pararescue jumpers, called PJs. While one of the helicopters hovered over Locher's location, a PJ was lowered on a hoist through the trees. He found Locher and helped him onto the hoist. The Jolly Green's crew then raised the hoist, bringing Locher and the PJ aboard.

Escaping over the mountains on a low, zig-zagging course, the A-1 pilots led the HH-53s back to Thailand. After three weeks on the run, surviving on rainwater and scavenging food in the forest, Locher had lost 15 pounds (7 kilograms), but he was alive and well. He got a rousing welcome home at his 555th Fighter Squadron's headquarters, Udorn Royal Thai Air Base, Thailand. For the Sandys and the Jolly Greens, it was all in a day's work.

Left: An Air Force pararescue jumper, and the aviator he has rescued, ride a hoist back aboard an HH-3 helicopter. This was a risky moment, as often the North Vietnamese Army or communist guerrilla fighters would ambush hovering choppers.

CHAPTER 3: Helicopter Pilots

Air Cavalry

Right: Air-mobile warfare in Vietnam helped change the face of modern combat. The infantry depended upon UH-1 Hueys (foreground) and the twin-rotor CH-47 Chinook (background) for supplies and transport.

The first helicopters were developed at the end of World War II (1939–1945). It was not until twenty years later, however, during the Vietnam War, that the military realized the full potential of helicopters. In Southeast Asia, chopper crews and their aircraft had a profound effect on the infantry combat tactics of both the Army and Marine Corps.

During the Korean War (1950–1953), the military used helicopters to develop tactics using the theory of "vertical envelopment." Vertical envelopment meant dropping or landing infantry behind and around an enemy to attack its rear and flanks. One of the most commonly used helicopters in the Vietnam War was the UH-1 Iroquois, also known as the "Huey." Army, Marine Corps, Navy, and Air Force crews flew the Hueys on transport, medical evacuation (MEDEVAC), and special-operations missions. Huey crews could transport seven combat-loaded infantrymen or three stretchers for wounded troops. On assault missions, UH-1 crews often flew into combat armed with two M60 0.3-inch (7.62-mm) machine guns mounted at the helicopter's side doors. Because helicopters were especially vulnerable to bullets and **shrapnel** during hover, landing, and takeoff, Huey pilots were trained to get their aircraft down onto the ground as rapidly as possible. In a development of the vertical envelopment theory, troops riding in the Huey jumped off and took up fighting positions around the helicopter. The troops unloaded supplies, loaded wounded men onto the helicopter, and defended the aircraft's fast exit. This tactic was known as "air assault."

AIR ASSAULT ON THE IA DRANG VALLEY

One of the most famous helicopter air assaults took place between October 18 and November 15, 1965, at the Ia Drang Valley in South Vietnam's Central Highlands. Along the river valley, the North Vietnamese and NLF had assembled a powerful

Right: A view over the shoulder of the door gunner of a gunship searching for targets in the Mekong Delta in 1968.

force of three army regiments—the 32nd, 33rd, and 66th—and a battalion of NLF troops. U.S. Army soldiers and Hueys of the Seventh Cavalry and the Fifth Cavalry air-assaulted the Ia Drang Valley, supported by two batteries of 4.1-inch (105-mm) howitzers from the First Battalion, Twenty-first Artillery. The U.S. force selected a landing zone that could accept ten Hueys at a time in order to bring in many troops quickly in case of trouble. The landing zone was code-named "X-Ray." There, Huey crews started to land the first wave of a battalion of cavalry troopers. It took many trips to chopper in all the U.S. troops and equipment.

In the middle of the air assault, the NVA suddenly attacked. The NVA outnumbered U.S. troops almost five to one. During the fight, at least two Hueys were hit by rifle, machine gun, and rocket-propelled grenade fire and crashed. As the fighting grew more intense, reinforcements from the Second Battalion, Seventh Cavalry and the Second Battalion, Fifth Cavalry made air assault landings on the NVA's flanks. The reinforcements fought through to join their comrades at Landing Zone X-Ray. With air and artillery support, the U.S. troops finally were able to push the larger NVA and NLF forces onto the defensive. A total of 79 U.S.

Below: The U.S. Army's air cavalry could use its Hueys to take the battle to remote areas that could not be reached by other vehicles.

soldiers were killed, with another 121 wounded during the battle. A U.S. Army report estimated that 581 NVA and NLF troops died. The battle at the Ia Drang Valley proved that an air assault force could be more effective than a larger force that did not have air mobility.

THE AH-1 HUEYCOBRA

The battle at Landing Zone X-Ray in the Ia Drang Valley also showed that the Huey, while effective as a troop transport, had its limitations. The UH-1 was just too slow and too wide a target to

Below: The AH-1 HueyCobra gunship, pictured here in the foreground escorting an unarmed Huey, was designed specifically for attacking ground targets.

be an effective gunship. Improving on the Huey's design, the Army in 1966 developed the two-seat AH-1 HueyCobra, the world's first attack helicopter. Pilots and gunners of the two-man HueyCobra gunship flew at twice the UH-1's speed and—because of a broader rotor and more powerful engine—could spend three times as long hovering in a combat zone. Armed with 2.75-inch (70-mm) rockets, 1.5-inch (40-mm) grenades, and machine guns, HueyCobra crews escorted Hueys to landing zones, adding covering fire as the infantry dismounted to fight.

At An Loc, South Vietnam, on March 30, 1972, Army HueyCobra crews were sorely tested. As NVA troops pushed south toward Saigon in what became known as the Easter Offensive, the communists smashed into the South Vietnamese city of An Loc with Soviet-built T-54 tanks, artillery, and infantry. Close air support was difficult at An Loc because the NVA brought in a new weapon: the Soviet-made SA-7 shoulder-launched missile. These small missiles could shoot down an aircraft by homing in on its hot exhaust. Despite the risk from these missiles, however, sixteen HueyCobras buzzed over the city just as the South Vietnamese and U.S. infantry forces, at An Loc were about to be overrun by enemy tanks. The HueyCobra crews dove straight down onto the T-54s, firing high-explosive rockets through the tanks' turrets. According to an Army report, U.S. and South Vietnamese forces wrecked eighty NVA tanks at An Loc, many of these attributed to the HueyCobra crews. By way of comparison, the NVA shot down only four AH-1s.

EVACUATION BY HELICOPTER

Helicopters played important roles at other dramatic moments during the Vietnam War. On April 7, 1975, Air Force, Marine Corps, and Navy helicopter pilots evacuated 82 U.S. personnel, 159 Cambodians, and other allies from the Cambodian capital,

Above: As the North Vietnamese Army closed in on Saigon in 1975, helicopters helped evacuate the U.S. Embassy.

Phnom Penh. Communist forces captured the city just as the U.S. helicopters escaped. On April 29, 1975, Navy, Marine Corps, and Air Force helicopter pilots, under Operation Frequent Wind, helped evacuate the city of Saigon. With communist forces shelling the city and the airport, helicopter pilots made hundreds of flights from the mobbed U.S. Embassy compound out to the ships of Navy Task Force 76 in the Gulf of Tonkin. The evacuation of Saigon went on for eighteen hours as helicopter crews rescued more than seven thousand South Vietnamese and

U.S. citizens. On April 30, 1975, just two hours after the last chopper lifted Marines away from the doomed city, NVA tanks crashed through the gates of Saigon's presidential palace, signaling the fall of South Vietnam.

"DUST OFF" MEDEVAC MISSIONS

Air ambulances were MEDEVAC helicopters dedicated to carrying wounded troops out of danger. Two pilots, a crew chief, and a medical corpsman manned the MEDEVAC choppers. Air ambulance choppers hovered in the air and used a hoist and litter to retrieve wounded personnel in places where the helicopter could not land, such as on forested hillsides. MEDEVAC choppers also made fast landings to load casualties directly. Because of dust raised by rotor downwash, rescue missions performed by MEDEVAC choppers were called "dust offs."

Left: Helicopters proved their worth when evacuating wounded men from the front lines. When minutes made the difference between life and death, MEDEVAC choppers helped tip the balance of the equation.

Rolling Thunder

Right: B-52 Stratofortress crews flew long missions from bases outside Vietnam. Until very late in the war, B-52 raids were restricted under a policy that many believe minimized the strategic effectiveness of early bombing **sorties**.

The heaviest airborne firepower brought down upon the NVA and NLF came from the crews of the Air Force's B-52 Stratofortress and F-105 Thunderchief bombers. During the Vietnam War, the United States dropped more than seven million tons of bombs on Southeast Asia, with two million tons of that total dropped along the Ho Chi Minh Trail. Although many bomber pilots flew over Vietnam from bases outside the war zone—at Thailand and Guam, for example—aircrews and ground crews were not isolated from danger. For instance, on the night of November 1, 1964, the NLF attacked Bien Hoa Air Base, near Saigon. The NLF attacked with mortar bombs that ignited the base's ammunition stores. The explosions killed four U.S airmen, destroyed five B-57 Canberra bombers, and damaged thirteen other planes.

On missions above the battlefields of Vietnam, the bomber crews did not face the same moment-to-moment horrors that soldiers saw in ground combat. Bomber crewmen, however, were in constant danger from surface-to-air missiles and antiaircraft artillery shells that could tear their planes apart. Additionally, bomber crewmen had to be on guard against North Vietnamese MiG interceptors.

OPERATION ROLLING THUNDER

The first strategic bombing campaign over Vietnam was called Operation Rolling Thunder. Between March 2, 1965, and November 1, 1968, Rolling Thunder raids attacked North Vietnamese military **infrastructure**. The F-105 Thunderchief, nicknamed the "Thud," was the workhorse of Rolling Thunder. Thuds could carry a heavy bomb load and were armed with a 0.79-inch (20-mm) cannon to defend themselves if attacked by MiGs. Many targets were located along heavily defended approaches to major cities, such as Hanoi and Haiphong. The first

Below: As well as its bomb load, the F-105 Thunderchief fighter-bomber (also known as the "Thud") was armed with a 0.79-inch (20-mm) cannon. Some pilots used their cannon to shoot down North Vietnamese fighter planes.

part of the journey to a target, such as a railroad bridge at Hanoi, might be uneventful. Once a Thud crossed into North Vietnamese airspace, however, the pilot braced for danger.

As he flew over Hanoi, the Thud pilot saw antiaircraft artillery fire flashing below him. Yellow and red tracer bullets, like strings of fireflies, burned up into the sky around the F-105. Hotter blue and white flashes came from heavier cannon. As the targeted railroad bridge came into view, the Thud pilot waited for his turn in the formation to start his attack run. Falling at more than 500 miles (805 km) per hour, the pilot steered the nose of his plane toward a section of the railroad bridge. At the proper elevation, the pilot pressed the "pickle" switch on his control stick to release his bombs. As the bombs struck and blasted apart a **buttressed**

span of the railroad bridge, the Thud pilot rolled the big jet over into a long, arcing turn and raced off toward Thailand. Coming out of the bombing run was more dangerous than going in, however, because the Thud pilot faced a now–alert gauntlet of antiaircraft batteries along the route to safety.

SURFACE-TO-AIR MISSILES

Of the 833 F-105s that had entered service with the Air Force by the end of the war, North Vietnamese antiaircraft artillery and surface-to-air missiles had downed 305. North Vietnamese fighter pilots claimed another sixteen. The worst threat facing the F-105 pilots, however, was the Soviet-built SA-2 Guideline surface-to-air missile. North Vietnamese SA-2 sites usually had six launchers, dug into protective earth pits in a 400-foot (122-m) ring around radar equipment. When the SA-2 site's radar equipment detected the height, range, and speed of a bomber flight, the North Vietnamese artillery crew launched Guideline missiles to intercept and destroy the planes. The missiles flew at more than three times the speed of sound, had a range of more than 25 miles (40 km), and had a maximum altitude of 60,000 feet (18,288 m).

SA-2s were not only dangerous to the Thuds—they also threatened the mightiest plane the Air Force bomber pilots flew: the B-52 Stratofortress. Air Force crews called a B-52 the "Big Ugly Fat Fellow," or the "BUFF." The BUFF was a massive, eight-engine bomber designed to carry nuclear weapons. Beginning in 1965, the Air Force used B-52s as conventional bombers, capable

TOUGH ODDS IN THE "THUD"

During the Vietnam War, a bomber pilot had to fly one hundred combat missions before he ended his tour of duty. Because of the threat from surface-to-air missiles and from antiaircraft artillery, Thunderchief pilots had a 75 percent chance of surviving one hundred missions. A mountainside along the North Vietnamese border was nicknamed "Thud Ridge" because so many damaged F-105s had crashed into it after being hit by enemy fire.

of carrying 30 tons (37 tonnes) of unguided bombs, known as "iron bombs," in a single **sortie**.

In Southeast Asia, B–52 crews flew missions code-named "Arc Light." Arc Light raids were planned as pinpoint attacks against NLF or NVA bases and supply depots. B–52 crews flew Arc Light raids from June 18, 1965, until August 15, 1973. The B–52s carried 108 bombs loaded into racks that ground crewmen fixed in the bomb bays and on **pylons** under each wing. Each B–52 crew could drop a staggering 60,000 pounds (27,216 kg) of **ordnance** in a single attack.

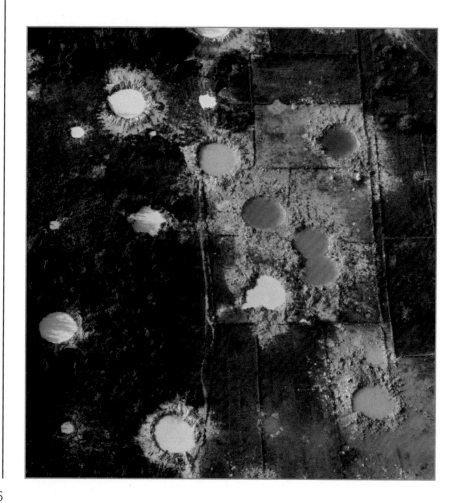

Right: The awesome power of aerial bombardment was revealed in the very landscape of Vietnam. The aftermath of a B-52 raid shows the deep impact craters left by the heavy bomb load these planes dropped.

SURVIVING A MISSILE HIT IN THE B-52

Left: The ground-radar-guided Russian-built SA-2 Guideline was a huge antiaircraft missile, feared by fighter and bomber crews alike.

Air Force Major John Wise, a B-52 pilot, recalled his 295th combat mission over Southeast Asia:

"We [dropped] our bombs. I put the B-52D into a 90-degree wingover when—Wham!—we were hit in the left side. All four engines on that side were finished. It was 250 miles [400 km] to reach friendly territory."

"We [decided] it was time to bail out. I called the gunner to go first. [Then] the navigator attempted to go, trying to blow the hatch below, but it did not open, probably jammed from the [missile] hit. The radar navigator ejected. I told the navigator to jump out the open radar navigator's hatch. The electronic warfare officer then ejected.

"At 3,000 feet [915 m] ... I squeezed the ejection handle [and] up and out I went. The chute opened with a jerk. I looked down to see the bomber hit the ground with a huge fireball."

37

OPERATION LINEBACKER I & II

In 1972, U.S. president Richard M. Nixon authorized Operation Linebacker, which was a new strategy designed to unleash the power of the B-52 on the North Vietnamese military. Linebacker was aimed at pressuring North Vietnam to accept a ceasefire. B-52 crews blasted every military base, supply depot, road, railway, port, and government facility north of the seventeenth parallel. B-52s pounded the cities of Hanoi and Haiphong and dropped sea mines in the latter's harbor, the most important in North Vietnam. In October of that year, Nixon stopped the bombing to allow U.S. diplomats time to meet with their North Vietnamese counterparts in Paris. When the Paris talks stalled, Nixon renewed the B-52 raids under Operation Linebacker II, which began December 18, 1972. During the eleven-day campaign, BUFF crews faced more than one thousand surface-to-air missiles and a storm of antiaircraft artillery fire. According to USAF figures, thirty-three airmen

Right: B-52s could carry vast amounts of ordnance in their internal bomb bays. To increase the bomb load still further, the Air Force also attached up to twenty-four bombs to the wing pylons—twelve examples of which are shown here.

Left: The B-52 was designed in the 1950s as a nuclear bomber capable of attacking targets in the Soviet Union. During the Vietnam War, the Air Force used these huge planes on conventional tactical strikes, decimating the North Vietnamese Army and its lines of supply.

were killed and fifteen B-52 aircraft destroyed. On December 29, 1972, the North Vietnamese finally agreed to accept the ceasefire. The agreement, signed in Paris on January 27, 1973, by officials from the United States and North and South Vietnam, was called

the Paris Accord. The accord officially ended the Vietnam War, although the war didn't actually end until April 30, 1975, when North Vietnam reunited the country under Communist control

Downed Pilots

Right: With a bayonet fixed to the muzzle of her rifle, this young North Vietnamese woman escorts a U.S. aircrewman, captured when he parachuted from his downed plane.

When a U.S. aircraft was hit by a surface-to-air missile or antiaircraft artillery fire or a MiG fighter, the aircrew had just seconds to react. If the damaged aircraft could not escape danger, the aircrew would attempt to eject and parachute away from their plane before it crashed into the ground. Ejecting from a jet at high speed is dangerous. The aviator pulled a black-and-yellow striped handle on his seat, and explosive charges blew off the airplane's canopy. A rocket then ignited under the seat, throwing the aviator out of the plane. The aviator was battered by g-forces and the wind as he flew out of his jet's cockpit. It was all over in a few seconds, and if he was lucky, the aviator would be left hanging from his parachute, watching his plane fall away in flames beneath him. When he landed—if he was not too badly injured—the aviator had to immediately hide himself from enemy infantry and local civilians who might have seen him drifting down in his parachute.

ESCAPE AND EVASION

Some aircrewmen were successful in escaping and evading the North Vietnamese. U.S. aircrews received survival training, which taught them how to find shelter, water, and food in the jungle. Each aircrewman carried a survival kit with a knife, a signal radio, basic medical supplies, and insect-proof netting. Some aircrewmen also carried a .38- or .45-caliber pistol for self-

SAM JOHNSON'S ORDEAL

U.S. Representative from Texas Sam Johnson recalled seven years as a prisoner of war in North Vietnam as a physically and psychologically challenging ordeal. Johnson was captured after being injured ejecting from his F-4 Phantom II.

"When I was captured I had a broken right arm, dislocated left shoulder and a broken back.... [My] jail cell in Hanoi had two other guys there when I went in. [We] were fed mostly pumpkin soup.

"Eleven of us were ... put in leg irons for two and a half years.... You learn a lot about yourself and how to survive in a POW camp."

41

INFAMOUS PRISONS

Prisons such as the "Zoo" and the "Hanoi Hilton" were infamous for the harsh treatment and barbaric living conditions prisoners suffered. The "Zoo," located southwest of Hanoi, had all the windows in the cells bricked up. The rooms were padlocked but had a slight crack that allowed prisoners to look out, or guards—and even prison livestock—to look in, which is how the prison got its nickname. U.S. aviators nicknamed North Vietnam's Hoa Lo prison (pictured) the "Hanoi Hilton." During their colonial rule over Vietnam, the French had called the prison Maison Centrale. Built by the French at the turn of the century, the prison was infested with rats, and some of the most brutal torture of Americans took place here in specially equipped rooms.

defense. Other aircrewmen, however, were unsuccessful. It was common for an aviator to be badly bruised, and even to suffer broken bones, when escaping his aircraft. A man with both arms fractured from a violent ejection was helpless once his parachute set him down. He lay where he fell, unable to get up, while his enemies closed in.

PRISON BRUTALITY

A captured aviator was moved to a prison or **internment** camp. At villages along the way, NVA soldiers used a megaphone to rouse local civilians, announcing that the captured man was one of many pilots that North Vietnam had shot down. From the North Vietnamese Communist party's point of view, U.S. aviators were "Yankee Air Pirates." The government in Hanoi considered those they captured to be war criminals. The North Vietnamese tried to convince captured aviators to appear in films or at press conferences, making statements against the war and denouncing the United States. The North Vietnamese government wanted to use prisoners' statements as propaganda. Prisoners were offered early release if they made statements against the U.S. war effort. Some agreed and were released. According to accounts from captured aviators, the North Vietnamese abused captive aircrewmen who refused.

U.S. military personnel assumed a chain of command in prison, with the most senior officer or rank taking the lead. U.S. aircrewmen were trained that, if captured, their first duty was to escape. Escape plans were approved through the prisoners' chains of command. The lead prisoner gave permission for an escape attempt. When an escape was unsuccessful, the consequences were brutal. The NVA troops sometimes killed recaptured escapees, according to some accounts. The prisoners who remained behind were often beaten or deprived of food and water as punishment for their roles in aiding the escapees. Guards used bamboo canes to whip a prisoner one hundred times a day for nine days, according to one survivor's account.

Because the NVA prison guards forbade talking, the prisoners developed other methods of communication. One method was a kind of Morse code that prisoners used to tap out letters of the alphabet. Communicating this way, captured aviators kept up morale, shared information about the outside world, and plotted their escape.

OPERATION HOMECOMING

A total of 591 U.S. aircrewmen were held captive in North Vietnam until 1973. For some of these men, their internment had lasted seven years. On February 12, 1973, Operation Homecoming began. A C-130 with medical personnel aboard landed at Gia Lam Airport, Hanoi. For the next six weeks, large C-141 Starlifter jet transports made the journey into North Vietnam, ferrying prisoners away to Clark Air Force Base in the Philippines and freedom. Because of their poor health, few of the freed prisoners returned to flight duty.

Time Line

1955: October, South Vietnam officially becomes the Republic of Vietnam (RVN).

1962: Military Assistance Command, Vietnam (MACV) established in Saigon.

1964: August, USS *Maddox* is reportedly attacked by North Vietnamese in Gulf of Tonkin; Congress passes the Gulf of Tonkin Resolution; U.S. aircraft bomb North Vietnamese targets.

1965: February, Operation Rolling Thunder begins; December, Operation Rolling Thunder is suspended in an attempt to bring North Vietnam to the negotiating table.

1966: January, Operation Rolling Thunder resumes.

1968: January, siege of Khe Sanh begins; April, Khe Sanh is relieved; November, Richard Nixon is elected president and commits the U.S. to a steady withdrawal from Vietnam.

1970: December, Congress repeals the Gulf of Tonkin Resolution.

1971: Major U.S. airstrikes are directed at North Vietnamese forces gathering to attack South Vietnam.

1972: NVA troops push into South Vietnam in the Easter Offensive but are driven back by heavy bombing; April, Operation Linebacker I begins; December 18–30, Operation Linebacker II is carried out, forcing the North Vietnamese to negotiate.

1973: January, peace accords are signed in Paris, France; February, Operation Homecoming begins as POWs are allowed to return home; March, last U.S. ground troops leave Vietnam.

1975: January, North Vietnam announces an all-out offensive to seize South Vietnam; April, last U.S. citizens are evacuated from Saigon; North Vietnamese take Saigon.

Glossary

artillery: large-barreled, crew-served mounted weapons

buttressed: supported or strengthened

fuselage: the body of an aircraft

head-up display: information projected into a pilot's field of vision so as to be visible without lowering the eyes

incendiary: designed to start fires

infantry: soldiers trained, armed, and equipped to fight on foot

infrastructure: the permanent installations required for military purposes; or the system of public works of a country, state, or region

internment: confinement or impoundment, especially during a war

ordnance: military supplies, including weapons, ammunition, combat vehicles, and maintenance tools and equipment

pylon: a rigid structure on the outside of an aircraft to which weapons or other stores may be attached

shrapnel: bomb, mine, or shell fragments

sortie: one mission or attack by a single plane

strafing: firing weapons at close range and especially with machine-gun fire from low-flying aircraft

Further Reading

BOOKS

Blesse, Maj. Gen. Frederick C. *Check Six: A Fighter Pilot Looks Back*. New York: Ballantine Books, 1992.

Churchill, Jan. *Hit My Smoke: Forward Air Controllers in Southeast Asia*. Manhattan, KS: Sunflower University Press, 1997.

Cook, John L. *Rescue under Fire: The Story of Dust Off in Vietnam*. Atglen, PA: Schiffer Publishing, 1998.

Dorr, Robert F. *Skyraider*. New York: Bantam Books, 1988.

WEB SITES

The Public Broadcasting System: American Experience
www.pbs.org/wgbh/amex/vietnam/
This online program has a timeline of the Vietnam War.

The U.S. Air Force Museum
www.wpafb.af.mil/museum/history/vietnam/vietnam.htm
This museum has an online exhibit of Vietnam War material and a timeline.

The POW Network
www.pownetwork.org
This network has information on prisoners of war and personnel missing in action.

The Air Force in Vietnam
www.airpower.maxwell.af.mil/airchronicles/aureview/
1983/jan-feb/dunn.html
This site presents official histories of Air Force personnel who served in Vietnam.

Index